Diary

Everything You Need to Know About

DATE RAPE

Dating can be a good way to get to know people.

Everything You Need to Know About

DATE RAPE

Frances Shuker–Haines

Series Editor: Evan Stark, Ph.D.

THE ROSEN PUBLISHING GROUP, INC.
NEW YORK

Published in 1990, 1992, 1995, 1998 by The Rosen Publishing Group, Inc.
29 East 21st Street, New York, NY 10010

Revised Edition 1998

Copyright © 1990, 1992, 1995, 1998 by The Rosen Publishing Group, Inc.

Library of Congress Cataloging-in-Publication Data

Shuker-Haines, Frances
    Everything you need to know about date rape / Frances Shuker-Haines.—revised
ed.
    (The Need to know library)
    Include bibliographical references and index.
    Summary: Explains what date rape is, how to avoid it, and where to find help if
you're a victim.
    ISBN 0-8239-2882-9
    1. Acquaintance rape—United States—Juvenile literature. [1. Acquaintance rape.
2. Rape. 3. Dating violence.] I. Title. II. Series.
HV6561.S56 1989
362.88'3   95-10702
                                                                                 CIP
                                                                                  AC

Manufactured in the United States of America

Contents

Introduction

Kelly was really excited when Derek asked her out. She always thought that he was cute, but she never thought he would be interested in her. He usually hung out with the really cool kids in their school.

Derek took her to a party at his friend's house. At the party, Kelly felt uncomfortable. She didn't know anybody there. Many kids were drinking or smoking.

Derek suggested they find someplace quiet where they could talk. He took Kelly into an empty room. Kelly was a little nervous to be alone with Derek, but he put her at ease, listening to Kelly talk about her dream of becoming a doctor. He truly seemed interested in what she had to say.

Then Derek pulled her into his arms and kissed her. Kelly was a little startled by his kiss, but she enjoyed it. They continued kissing but then Kelly felt Derek's hand unbuttoning her shirt. Kelly brushed his hand away and suggested they take a break and talk.

"I think we've talked enough," Derek said. "Let's have some fun."

Derek pushed her to the floor and got on top of her. His hands were all over her. She was getting scared.

"Derek, stop, I don't want to do this," Kelly said to him. But Derek didn't stop. It was as if he didn't hear what she was saying. His hand was up her skirt. "Derek, no! Stop!" Kelly shouted. She couldn't move. She tried pushing him, but he was so heavy. Kelly kept shouting no and telling him to stop. But he wouldn't stop.

Many people have the mistaken idea that a person can be raped only by a stranger. But what Derek did to Kelly is also considered rape. Derek date-raped Kelly.

Date rape occurs when two people get together socially and one person forces the other to have sex. No matter what kind of relationship the two people have, no one has the right to force another to have sex against his or her will. It doesn't matter if the two people are dating, married, or even if they've had sex before. Just because a person agrees to go on a date with another person, it doesn't mean that he or she wants to have sex with that person.

Unfortunately date rape is not a rare occurrence. According to the National Victim Center, one out of every eight adult women has been raped. Four out of every five rape survivors know their rapists.

Being raped is a traumatic experience, but when a person is raped on a date, it can be more difficult because the rapist is someone the victim knows and trusted enough to go out on a date with. The victim may also have to see the assailant at school every day.

Rape victims also must decide whether or not to report the attack. This is a personal choice, and there is no right or wrong decision, but it is especially harder for victims of date rape. The survivors may fear other people's reactions. They may feel that others are less likely to believe them—especially if the attacker is someone popular and thought of as a "nice" person.

Rape victims experience many different emotions after an attack. They feel shame, confusion, fear, and even guilt. They may wonder if they somehow caused the rape. But it's extremely important to know that rape is never the victim's fault. No one has the right to force you to have sex if you don't want to. Rape is a violent crime.

This book will discuss date rape and some of the reasons why it happens. This book will also dispel the myths and stereotypes that many people have about rape with truth and facts. In addition to the physical consequences of date rape, rape victims also are psychologically affected by a rape. This book will discuss what to do if you are raped and how to help a friend who is raped. Finally this book will discuss several methods you can use to protect yourself and lessen the chances of becoming a rape victim.

A note about the language in this book: A victim is anyone who is raped, but that person is also called a survivor. This book refers to people who have been raped as both victims and survivors. This book usually refers to survivors as "she," and assailants as "he," but both females and males can be raped. And though most assailants are males, females also commit rape.

Chapter 1

"Date" and "Rape": Why Have They Come Together?

Date rape is not a new problem; it is only a new term. It may be hard to believe that women and girls can be raped by their dates, since most of us think of rape as something a man does to a person he does not know. In movies or on TV we see rapists stalking their victims through dark alleys.

The fact is that 80 percent of all reported rapes are *acquaintance rapes*, or rapes that happen between people who already know each other. *Date rape* occurs when two people go on a date and the man forces the woman to have sex when she doesn't want to. There is always a risk of date rape, even if two people have dated before.

In our culture, a date can sometimes lead to sex. Some people go on dates simply because they hope to have sex. No matter how polite a date may seem, he could become frustrated and violent if he does not get what he was after. Remember, *any* kind of forced sex is rape.

Myth and Truth

"Look at the way she's dressed. She's just asking for trouble."

"What was she doing alone with him? She's partly to blame."

"He's such a nice guy, I can't believe he would rape anybody."

These are some of the false myths that some people believe about rape. Rape is a violent crime, but many people make false assumptions about rapists and victims. Their assumptions often come from their belief of the myths that surround rape. A myth is an idea or story that many people believe in, but more often than not, the myth is false.

There are many myths surrounding rape. In this section, we will list some common myths and then discuss how these myths are false.

- **A woman can be only raped by a stranger with a weapon who lurks in dark alleys.** This idea is false. A majority of rape survivors are attacked by people they know, such as a friend, a date, or even a husband.
- **A woman is only playing "hard to get" when she says no.** When a woman says no, she means no. Guys need to respect a woman's decision.
- **Men rape only when they don't get enough sex.** When a man rapes, he does not want sex.

The victim needs support from friends who will believe her and listen to her problems.

Rape is a violent crime committed by a person who craves power and control over someone else.

- **Date rape doesn't exist. Girls claim rape only because they feel guilty about having sex.** Anytime someone forces another to have sex against her will, it is rape. It doesn't matter if they know each other or are on a date. Very few women lie about being raped.
- **Once a girl has agreed to have sex with a guy, she can never say no to him again.** A woman has the right to say no at any time, no matter what their previous sexual relationship.
- **It's always the woman's fault if she is raped.** Rape is a crime and is never the victim's fault. Like all crimes, the criminal is at fault.
- **A woman who flirts with a man means she wants to have sex with him.** When two people go out on a date, they want to have a good time and enjoy each other's company. Flirting is a fun part of dating, but a woman who flirts with a man is not signaling that she wants to have sex.
- **If a man spends a lot of money on a date, he is entitled to have sex with her.** Nothing a man does or how much money he spends entitles a man to sex. Sex takes places between two consenting adults. If a woman is forced to have sex against her will, it is rape.
- **Boys are rarely raped.** Anyone can be a victim of rape—men, women, children, homosexuals, and heterosexuals.

- **A woman who dates a lot of men, wears sexy clothing, and stays out late has no one to blame but herself if she is raped.** No matter how a person acts or dresses, it doesn't mean she has no control over her body. Nobody has the right to force her to do something she doesn't want to.
- **A woman who goes someplace alone with a man must be willing to have sex with him.** In a romantic relationship, it's perfectly natural and acceptable to want to spend time together. However, a woman who wants to be alone with a man does not mean she wants to have sex with him.
- **A person can never return a normal life after being raped.** Although being raped is a highly traumatic experience, a person can recover from it and live a happy and fulfilling life.

We have mentioned only some of the myths that surround rape. The one truth to keep in mind is that no matter what the circumstances, no one has the right to force another to engage in sexual activities against his or her will.

Being raped is physically and emotionally damaging, especially if someone is raped by a person she thought she could trust. One basic human right is that a person has the right over his or her body. When that right is violated, the person feels as if he or she has no control over anything. Physical injuries heal, but emotional scars can last for a long time. Rape is a violent crime. Survivors of rape need understanding and support.

Sometimes boys feel pressure to trade stories about girls.

Chapter 2

From Dream Come True to Nightmare

Jeff was one of the popular guys. He was a good-looking soccer player, and he always seemed to have a swarm of admirers around him, male and female. Sandy would watch him when he wasn't looking.

She was fascinated with Jeff. He always acted really tough, but she could sense that there was a sensitive, vulnerable side to him that most people did not see. Sandy wanted to meet him and to get to know him better. But she could not seem to get past the circle of worshiping fans who always surrounded him. He was like a celebrity, so far out of reach for her. Besides, he seemed to be interested only in popular blondes with big hair and no opinions. That was why she was so excited when Jeff suddenly asked her to the dance on Friday night. She'd been

hoping he would ask. Maybe this would be the
beginning of something. Maybe she would be Jeff's
new girlfriend! Sandy couldn't wait until Friday.

All that week, Sandy flirted with Jeff after
school. As far as Sandy could tell, they both
seemed pretty excited about their date. She just
hoped she wouldn't blow it somehow. Oh well,
nothing to do now but wait and see, she thought.

When Friday night rolled around, Sandy and her
friends headed out for the school. They were
meeting the guys there. Sandy had spent hours
trying on outfits. She finally felt pretty good about
how she looked. She just hoped Jeff would like
her too.

When they got to school, Jeff took one look at
her and let out a slow whistle. Sandy was
embarrassed. After all, their friends were there.
But she figured it was a compliment and she
should be flattered. She just smiled and blushed.
Jeff took her hand and led her inside.

The school gym was packed. The band was
playing full blast. Jeff was a great dancer. Sandy
was really enjoying dancing with him. A slow song
came on and Jeff pulled her close. She could smell
beer on his breath. The guys must have gone to
the lake before the dance and had a few. Sandy
didn't like beer much. But she figured, "boys will
be boys," as her mother used to say. She felt Jeff's
hands on her back, and then even lower. He was

pulling her toward him and pushing himself into her. It was kind of exciting. But it was kind of scary and embarrassing, too. Jeff was really pressuring her. Sandy started to feel more and more uncomfortable. After all, they were in the middle of the school! Her English teacher was right across the room!

Sandy started to pull away. Jeff looked in her eyes. "Relax," he said. "Don't be so uptight. Just enjoy yourself." But it wasn't that easy for Sandy. She wanted him to stop. But she couldn't bring herself to tell him. Then he might not want to date her again. Then she definitely *wouldn't* be his next girlfriend. At last, the song was over. Sandy rushed to the girls' room to find her best friend, Sarah. But she wasn't there. Oh well, at least Jeff really liked her, she thought. It was probably just the beer that made him act so bold in front of everybody.

Jeff was waiting for her outside the girls' room. "Let's get out of here. It's too crowded," he said. "But I'm supposed to go home with my friends," said Sandy. "I promised my parents." "Don't worry," said Jeff. "I'll get you home." "Well," said Sandy, "I really think I'd better find my friends. I should go home with them like I promised." "Hey don't you trust me?" asked Jeff. "I said I'd get you home, didn't I?" "Okay," said Sandy finally. She was a little worried about going off alone with Jeff. But she didn't want their date to end so soon.

So she took his hand, and they walked outside. "Where are we going?" asked Sandy. "How about the lake?" said Jeff. Sandy knew a lot of kids went to the lake to make out. And it sure would be fun to make out with Jeff. Wow, was he cute! "Okay," said Sandy. "Great," said Jeff. "I know a special spot where no one will bother us."

When they got to the lake, Jeff led Sandy to a patch of woods nearby. He sat down by a big mossy tree trunk and pulled on Sandy's hand. She lost her balance and landed smack in his lap. She giggled a little at that. Jeff reached around the tree and pulled out a six-pack of beer. "I hid these here before the dance," he said proudly. So, Sandy thought, he just assumed I'd come here with him! She felt a little funny about that. Then she thought maybe it was supposed to be a compliment. It proved he really liked her.

Jeff opened two beers and handed her one. "Uh, I don't really like beer," said Sandy. "You're kidding!" said Jeff. "I don't believe you. Come on, try it. Give it another chance." "Okay," said Sandy. "But I don't think I'm going to like it." Jeff started chugging his beer. Then he crushed the can in his bare hand. He was definitely showing off for her. He leaned over to kiss her. It was great. Except for the beer on his breath, he was a really good kisser. "Hey," he said between kisses.

Dancing close does not mean a girl wants sex.

"Where'd you learn to kiss like that?" Sandy couldn't believe it—he actually thought *she* was a good kisser. Amazing.

Pretty soon, Jeff started to put his hand under her sweater. Sandy wasn't sure she wanted him to do that, but she was afraid to say "no"and spoil the evening. So she let him. But then he started to get carried away. His hands were all over her. "Hey!" she said. "What do you think you're doing?" But he wouldn't stop.

Before she knew it, he was taking down her underpants. "Jeff, wait!" she said. "Come on, let's slow down." But he didn't seem to be listening. He got on top of her. "Jeff, stop!" cried Sandy. "Relax," he said. "You'll enjoy it."

"No, Jeff! Don't!" Sandy had never dreamed she would be having sex with Jeff. She barely knew him. She wasn't ready yet. She didn't have birth control. She just didn't *want* to.

"Jeff, please don't. Stop. Jeff? Please?" But all his weight was on her. He was inside her. It was over in a few seconds.

Sandy started to cry. "Hey, what's wrong?" said Jeff. "I thought we were having fun." Sandy was too stunned to say anything. She pulled her underpants up. Finally she managed to blurt out, "I want to go home now." "No problem," said Jeff. They walked home in silence. When they got to her front door, Jeff tried to kiss her. "You better not," said Sandy. "My dad's watching." "I'll call you," said Jeff. Sandy ran inside her house.

Sandy didn't tell anyone what had happened to her. She wasn't *sure* what had happened to her.

Why had Jeff gone ahead when she hadn't wanted him to? What had she done? Maybe she shouldn't have gone to the lake. But she'd wanted to kiss Jeff. Wasn't that all right? Maybe she shouldn't have kissed him so passionately. After all, maybe he just couldn't help himself. Maybe she shouldn't have let him put his hands under her sweater. But she knew that what he'd done after that had been wrong.

In her mind, she kept seeing Jeff on top of her. He barely knew she was there. She was just some *thing* to him. He didn't care about her. How could she have been so wrong about him? And how could she ever face him now? He'd acted like there was nothing wrong. *Was* she making something out of nothing? She was confused, unsure. Well, one thing was certain. She wasn't going to school on Monday. She just needed to be alone for a while to figure everything out.

When Sandy's friends called to ask her about her date, she lied. "Oh, it was fun," she said. She just couldn't bring herself to tell them what Jeff had done. Besides, she thought it might be her fault. She didn't want her friends to give her a hard time about being a "slut." But Sandy's best friend, Sarah, could tell that something was wrong. When Sandy didn't show up for school on Monday, Sarah got worried. She went to Sandy's house after school.

Sarah could tell Sandy had been crying. "Sandy, what happened? What's wrong?" asked Sarah.

"Nothing. I'm just not feeling well."

"What happened on Friday night? I expected you to call Saturday morning. Didn't it work out with Jeff?"At that, Sandy burst into tears, and told Sarah everything."What did I do wrong?"she asked.

"Nothing! Jeff is a jerk!" said Sarah.

"Why do I feel so terrible?" cried Sandy.

"I don't mean to shock you," said Sarah. "But it sounds to me like you've been raped."

And that is, in fact, what had happened to Sandy. She had been raped. But she had some trouble seeing it that way. She couldn't believe that someone she knew and trusted could rape her. She assumed that bad things don't happen to "nice" girls. So she blamed herself. But she was wrong. No one deserves to be raped. Victims should not be blamed for the crime that was committed against them.

Jeff assumed that Sandy wanted sex because she had been flirting with him. He also assumed she wanted sex because *he* wanted it. He assumed she wanted sex because she came to the lake with him.

But Jeff was wrong. If a woman says "no," she means "no." No one should ever force someone else to have sex against their will. That's rape. And rape is the fault of the rapist, not the victim.

Chapter 3

Why Do Men Rape?

Nobody is truly certain why rape happens. Some say our society teaches men to rape. Others believe just the opposite—that men are naturally violent and that society is what keeps them from committing rape.

It is important to avoid the temptation of pointing the finger at a single factor, such as the media or pornography, as the cause for something as complicated as rape. But looking at how our society views men and women can give us an idea of what rape is really about.

Guns and Dolls

If you are a girl, you may have been given baby dolls to play with when you were little. If you are a boy, you probably grew up playing with footballs and toy guns. Have you ever wondered why? These toys show us *stereotypes* of boys and girls.

Stereotypes are commonly held beliefs that may or may not be true. They often lead us to assume things about girls and boys that are not true.

Stereotypes about boys usually focus on aggression and action. For example, many people believe that *all* boys like sports. Many boys do like sports, but there are also many who do not. And there are girls who like sports. Many people believe that all boys like to fight, or that boys should solve their problems by using violence. This also is not true.

Stereotypes about girls often show them as passive and weak, not strong and assertive. Girls are expected to be nurturing and emotional, but these are qualities that males can have as well. Seeing women as weak and helpless is one way of stereotyping them as victims.

These stereotypes influence the way young men and women perceive themselves and each other. This can lead to problems when they begin dating. Boys may believe that they are supposed to want sex all the time. They may also believe that girls are weak and will have sex with them whether they want to or not. These false beliefs can sometimes lead to date rape.

Girls often share these beliefs. For example, if a boy is being too aggressive, the girl may not tell him to stop even if she is uncomfortable because she has been taught that it is okay for boys to be aggressive. And if he becomes violent and tries to rape her, she may not know how to fight back because, over the years, she has been taught that girls are not supposed to fight.

Some boys think it is "macho" to date lots of girls.

We all know that women have come a long way toward equality. There are more and more women doing the jobs that used to be only done by men. But that doesn't mean that all the bad stereotypes about men and women are gone. Women do compete with men in the workplace. But many women think they are still supposed to be more passive when it comes to dating. Think about it: When it comes to making plans for a date who still makes the first phone call? Most of the time, it's the guy. And even though women can now wear suits to work, they are still supposed to look somewhat "sexy." But not *too* sexy. Many people

Girls are often taught that they must be pretty and obedient to attract boys.

will "blame" a woman if she is dressed in a certain way. They will think that somehow, a woman is "asking for trouble."

Date rape happens because many guys believe these ideas. They believe they should fight to get what they want (in this case, sex). They believe that "real men" have a lot of sex when they are young. They believe that women are passive, so they must be forced into having sex.

When guys "listen" to these stereotypes instead of to their dates, they are in danger of committing date rape. When a guy *expects* to have sex on a date, he is forgetting that there's another person involved. And that other person has a right to choose whether or not to have sex. A guy who believes the stereotypes will ignore his date's signals. He will stop listening to what she's saying. He will assume he knows what's best for her.

Think about Jeff. All his friends admired him. They knew he had sex with lots of girls. It was important to Jeff to be a big shot to his friends. So, he clearly expected to have sex with Sandy. He planted the beer at the tree. He made sexual advances all night. He ignored her hints that she might be uncomfortable. He made sure the date ended in sex, even though Sandy said no. He assumed she didn't mean it. He assumed she didn't mean it because she had come to the lake with him. Jeff raped Sandy because of the "lessons" he'd learned about girls and boys and sex.

Think about Sandy. She didn't want to dance so close to Jeff, but she was afraid to say no. She thought if she said no, Jeff wouldn't like her. She thought that she should please Jeff. She wanted to avoid conflict.

Sandy was surprised when Jeff pulled out the beers. Clearly he assumed she would come to the lake with him. He thought she couldn't make her own decisions. She didn't like having no choice in the matter.

She also didn't like it when he put his hand under her sweater. But Sandy was afraid to tell him. She wanted Jeff to like her. When Jeff raped her, she knew something bad had happened. But she didn't blame Jeff at first. She blamed herself. She thought she must have "asked" for it. She couldn't believe someone she liked and trusted could do this to her.

The Role of the Media

The media (movies, television, magazines, and advertisements) play an important role in how society sees women. The media often show women in stereotypical roles. They are shown as weak and submissive or as objects or property owned by men. Think of the last movie you saw, or the last magazine you flipped though, or the last commercial you saw. How are women shown? Do they often wear very revealing clothing or always seem to need men to rescue them from a dangerous enemy? What kind of role do they play other than to stand there and look beautiful? These images often send a message to society that women are weak and do not have minds of their own.

If a girl feels uncomfortable, she should speak up for herself.

Women are helpless. In most action movies and TV shows, the men are the ones out chasing the bad guys and saving the world. Where are the women? Often, they are victims. And it's up to the men to help them or save them. Sometimes the women are the beautiful girlfriends of the men, standing around and looking pretty. They are often thought of as *possessions* that the men have, like a sportscar or a gun. In movies and television, the women often don't *do* anything but support the men. The women are seen as entirely passive.

Women are sexual objects. Pornographic magazines (magazines with "dirty" pictures in them) are full of pictures of naked women. They are there to give men sexual pleasure. That's all. They are not shown as real people. They do not talk or have opinions. They are simply sexual objects. Many men consider these women to be the "ideal." They have been taught that the best woman is one that has no voice or personality. But women *are* people, not objects. And women (like all people) deserve respect.

Women's bodies are like products. Advertising uses pictures of beautiful women to sell products. For example many companies show women's legs to sell cigarettes? Advertising like this promotes two false ideas: That buying a certain product will "get" you a beautiful woman. And that you can "get" a beautiful woman as easily as you can buy a pack of cigarettes. Neither of these things are true!

It doesn't matter how much money you spend on a date. It doesn't matter how much you want a woman's body. It's her body, and she has the right to decide what she does with it, with whom, where, and when. Many people are bombarded with images from the media in their everyday lives.

Almost every American home has at least one television set. More and more people are going out to watch movies. We can't go outside without seeing an ad in a billboard. Some boys and girls may have a hard time telling the difference between the images shown on the media and real life. But it's important people to realize that the images seen in the media are not real. They often do not show real-life situations. Often these images are used to sell a product. Look around at the people you know. Do they look, act, or talk like the people seen in movies, television, or ads?

Despite what the media show, women are not objects to be bought and owned. Rape occurs when men stop seeing women as people and instead see them as objects.

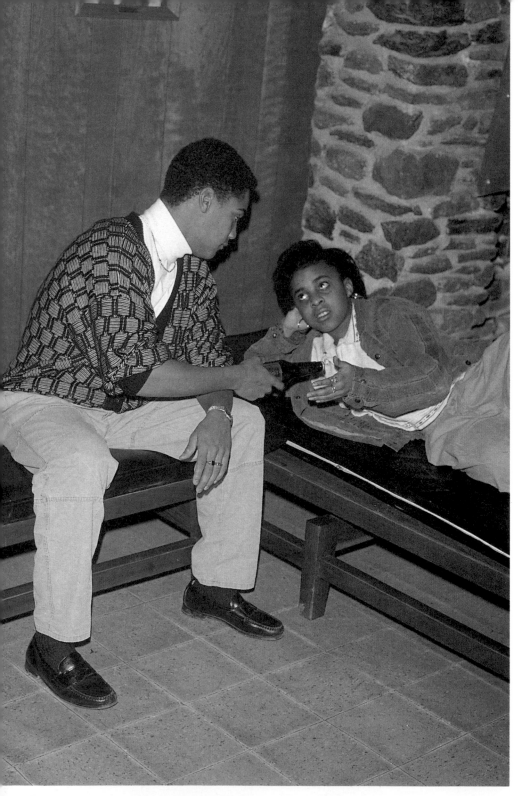

Just because a girl goes somewhere alone with a boy, it does not mean she wants to have sex with him.

Chapter 4

Self-Defense, Self-Empowerment

In the past 30 years, women have taken great strides toward equality. As women have learned to compete in a man's world, taking care of themselves and living independently, they have also had to learn to defend themselves in a way that only men once did. More women began to take self-defense classes and carry weapons. This type of responsibility comes with greater freedom.

This chapter is about how you, as a young woman, can protect yourself as you begin dating. Let's look at Sandy's situation again. One thing she could have done differently was *speak up for herself*. She did not like what Jeff was doing during the slow dance. She pulled away from him when she felt uncomfortable, but then gave in. She also didn't feel very good about not going home with her friends. But she was afraid Jeff wouldn't like her. So she went along with him, even though it made her uncomfortable. She didn't like beer, but she let Jeff talk her into drinking some. She didn't want Jeff to put his hands under her sweater, but she let him anyway.

Rape is a violent crime, it is a criminal act. Like other crimes of violence, there's the potential that it can happen to any of us. While there are steps that we can take to protect ourselves, ultimately it's something that may happen no matter what we do. But there were things that Sandy could have done differently to better protect herself from becoming a victim of rape.

Sandy made the mistake of thinking that Jeff was above her because he was popular and hung out with the popular people in school. She had low self-esteem. She didn't want to do anything to "blow it" with Jeff. She changed herself to please him. During their date, Sandy did things that she really didn't want to do, but did them anyway because she wanted to please Jeff. But if Sandy had confidence in herself and valued herself, she would have stood up to him.

But this does not justify what Jeff did to her. Jeff raped Sandy, and there is no excuse for that. But even if Sandy stood up for herself, there is no guarantee that Jeff wouldn't have raped her. Jeff was a school-mate, Sandy knew and trusted Jeff. Sandy had no reason to think that Jeff would hurt her.

Date rape is much more likely to happen when people have been drinking. It makes the rapist less sensitive.

Another way that Sandy could have protected herself was to have a backup method of getting home instead of relying on Jeff. She was stuck with Jeff at the lake. Maybe if she'd had another way of getting home she could have left when things got uncomfortable. Sandy also could have asked Jeff not to drink alcohol. Alcohol is a drug. Not only is alcohol illegal for those under twenty-one, but it can also cloud a person's judgment. It can make some people act in ways they normally would not—including rape.

How to Protect Yourself

Although there are methods you can use to protect yourself and reduce the chances of becoming a rape victim, the bottom line is that anyone can be a victim of date rape.

- Avoid being alone with a guy you don't know or trust completely. A guy will not rape with other people around.
- Try to establish how far you will go sexually before the date. Ask the guy what he expects from the

date. If the guy is expecting something you're not going to do, don't go out with him.

- Exercise some caution about what you will wear on the date. Some guys will take advantage of a girl according to her outfit.
- Don't drink alcohol or be with a guy who is drinking or drunk. Alcohol can cloud a person's judgment, making him do things he normally would not. Another substance recently used in many cases of date rape is a drug known as Rohypnol. It is a powerful sedative that can cause someone to lose consciousness and can cause memory loss. Rohypnol dissolves easily in liquid, so keep an eye on your drink and don't accept drinks from people you don't know or trust.
- If a guy starts pushing you to go farther sexually, use a firm and loud voice to say "No!" If you have to, yell, even if no one is around.
- Follow your instincts. If something feels wrong, just walk away.

Chapter 5

Attention, Guys: How You Can Prevent Rape

John had never had sex. His friends always made fun of him for being a virgin, and he really wanted to prove to them that he could do it. So he decided to go out with Maria. From what he had heard, she never turned anybody down for sex. It was the perfect opportunity to get it over with and get his friends off his back.

When he picked her up at her apartment, Maria was wearing very tight pants with platform shoes and a tight, revealing pink sweater. She looked fabulous, like a young model. She smiled flirtatiously and said, "Hello, darling!" Then she grabbed his hand and kissed him on the mouth. "It's a beautiful night, love. Let's go for a walk before we hit the nightclubs!" She kissed me, John thought. She can't wait! While they were walking, Maria kept stroking his palm with

her fingers. Occasionally they'd stop and kiss.
Maria had this unbelievable way of nibbling on his
ear. By the time they got to the club, John was
super excited. He ordered a large frozen margarita.
Maria, he noticed, was only having Coca-Cola. Oh,
well, maybe she didn't *need* to drink, he thought.
This dating/sex thing is probably routine for her.
But he felt that he might lose his cool if he didn't
have something to calm himself down. By the time
the music was over, John had downed three
margaritas. He felt much more confident. He was
ready for the real excitement to begin.

   He took Maria to his friend Freddie's
apartment—Freddie's parents were away for the
weekend. The minute they closed the door, Maria
was all over him. She was an incredible kisser.
They ended up on the floor. Well, now's my
chance, thought John. He started to undress
Maria. When he started unzipping her pants, she
whispered, "No, John. Not now. Let's save that
for another time." "Oh, I see," said John. "You're
playing hard to get. Well, you don't have to
pretend with me, Maria." "No, I mean it. Don't.
Let's just have fun doing what we're doing." John
was sure he knew what *that* meant. So he pulled
off her pants. "John, I said no," Maria repeated.
"Let's just kiss or something." "Yeah," said John.
"Or *something*!" He got on top of her. He *knew* she
didn't mean it. All the guys said she was easy.

It is important to treat your date with respect.

There was no way that she meant what she was saying. It was obvious that she'd been thinking about sex all night.

It was strange. The whole time he was having sex with her, she kept saying she didn't want to. She stopped kissing him. She was being really cold. And when they were through, she said, "I think I'd better be going," and before he knew it, she was out the door. What had gone wrong? Why hadn't she enjoyed the sex? And why did she keep saying no when it was so *obvious* that she was hot for him?

The fact is, John raped Maria, and didn't even know it. His head was so full with what he *thought* would happen, that he couldn't see what was really happening.

One of the strangest things about date rape is that sometimes men commit date rape without knowing what they've done. A burglar knows that he or she has stolen something. A car thief knows that he or she is taking someone else's car. A rapist in the bushes knows that he intends to rape someone.

But when it comes to date rape, things aren't that clear-cut. A lot of guys honestly believe the media stories we talked about earlier. They think that women really do mean "yes" when they say "no." They think that a woman must want sex if she goes somewhere alone with a guy. They think that if a girl flirts with a guy, she must want sex. They think that a girl owes a guy sex if he's spent a lot of money on her. So, when a guy like this forces his date to have sex, he may not even know he's raping her! He thinks he's just doing what guys are supposed to do on dates.

Well, we know better now. But let's think about ways we can be sure we don't make this kind of mistake in the future. For example, what could John in the story have done differently?

First of all, John could have *listened to his date.* When Maria said "no," he should have believed her and stopped—no matter how excited he was. It doesn't matter how sexy she actcd. Or think about the first story. Jeff could have "listened" to Sandy's signals all night. When Sandy pulled away from him at the dance, Jeff should have asked if she was uncomfortable. When Sandy said she wanted to go home with her friends, he shouldn't have talked her out of it. Both John and Jeff made all the decisions. Maria and Sandy couldn't make any. That's not fair.

Another thing both John and Jeff could have done was *not drink alcohol.* When you're drunk, you can't think very clearly. You might not notice the hints your date is sending you. You might let yourself "get carried away." If you *stay sober,* you can avoid tragic mistakes like date rape.

John shouldn't have expected to have sex on the date. Date rape often happens because the guy

Calling a rape crisis counselor can help you understand what has happened.

expects to have sex long before the date even happens. Maybe he's been thinking about it for days. Maybe he's planned the whole evening so it will end up with sex. John asked Maria out just so he could have sex with her. He clearly expected to have sex with her. He "knew" that she would want it, long before he even asked her. Well, you can't make plans for two people all by yourself. *Don't expect sex from your date.* Try to enjoy whatever happens. Remember, the point of dating is to have fun, and to find out if you and your date really like each other. The point of a date is not rape. Don't let yourself be a rapist.

Don't let yourself believe the lies you see in the media. Women are just as important as men. When guys forget that, it can lead to date rape. Remember, women are people. They aren't just something pretty to look at or have. And how they look doesn't mean they are ready for sex. Just because Maria had on tight pants doesn't mean she wanted sex. Sure, she wanted John to be attracted to her, but that doesn't mean she wanted him to force sex on her. When you see those lies about women in the media, make a point of noticing. Talk about it with your friends—male and female. Think about most of the women you know. They're not like the women in magazines or on TV, are they? They have minds of their own. They have personalities and opinions. They are people, not things. They deserve respect.

Guys can also be pressured into having sex against their will.

Chapter 6

Guys Can Be Victims, Too

Michael was a good-looking guy who was shy with girls. He had entered school in the middle of the year because his parents moved. He missed his old girlfriend from his old home town. They had agreed to break up when he moved. But he was still in love with her. He couldn't imagine being with anyone else.

That's why Michael was really surprised when Kathy asked him out. She was captain of the girls' basketball team—tall, athletic, and very outgoing. "We were talking about you at practice the other day," she said. "We decided you were very mysterious. So, I thought I'd better find out for myself what you were all about." Michael was flattered, but also very nervous. She was so popular and pretty! Why did she want to go out with *him?*

On their date they went to the movies. Then Kathy invited him to her apartment. No one else was home. She started coming on very strong, kissing him, stroking him. She was very hard to resist. "Well, the girls were right," she said. "You *do* have great lips!" She laughed.

Were they really talking about me this way, thought Michael? Wow! Kathy guided his hand under her shirt. Michael couldn't help himself—he started thinking about his old girlfriend and how much he missed her. Sure, it was nice being with Kathy, but he barely knew her. Before he knew it, Kathy was taking off his clothes and her clothes, scattering them around the room. Michael was suprised. Did this mean she wanted to have sex? He wasn't ready for that. He was still in love with his old girlfriend. *That's* who he wanted to be with, not Kathy.

"Um, Kathy," he stammered. "Do you think this is a good idea?" "Oh, give me a break, Michael. I'm giving you a chance of a lifetime! What's the problem?" She was laughing at him. "Well, I don't want to do this," he said. "I'm just not into it right now." "Oh, come *on,*" she said. "You've got to be kidding!" And before he knew it, she was all over him. "What's the matter,

Michael? You gay or something?" She laughed again.

She held him down and pulled his clothes off. Michael was embarrassed. He was actually trying to get away, but he couldn't. She did things to him that no girl had ever done to him before. He could not even enjoy having sex because he felt so confused and humiliated.

He could not figure out how this could have happened to him. He had never been like most of the guys he knew. He was not very macho and was always very considerate of girls' feelings. Kathy took advantage of his gentle disposition and forced him to have sex against his will. Michael had been raped.

Women are not usually the aggressors in rape, but sometimes it does happen. Men can be raped by women. And men can be raped by other men, too. Date rape can happen between gay men. If you are a man and know you have been raped by a woman or another man, do not be ashamed to get help. Talk to a counselor or a friend you trust.

What has happened to you is *not* your fault. And it does not make you any less of a man.

Anyone—man or woman—who forces another person to have sex against his or her will has committed rape.

Rape victims often feel alone. They blame themselves.

Chapter 7

What If It Happens to You?

If you are a victim of date rape, you will probably feel very confused and upset. A lot of different thoughts will be running through your head. Here are some of the things you might find yourself wondering:

How could this happen to me?

Sometimes we don't want to believe that something so horrible could happen to us. We try to find a reason for it. Rape victims often blame themselves. They think they must have done something wrong. That isn't true. It's not your fault if you were raped. It is the rapist's fault. You can (and should) be angry with him. Don't be angry with yourself.

How could he have done this to me?

We date people we think we like. We date people we think are nice. That makes it hard to believe that something as horrible as rape really happened. But even guys you think are nice can rape. There was no way for you to know what was going to happen. It's not your fault that your date ignored your wishes. *He's* the one at fault.

How can I ever trust anyone else again?

You trusted your date. He raped you. It's hard to feel good about people after an experience like that. But just because one person is bad doesn't mean that *everyone* is bad. Maybe there were some danger signals you didn't pick up on. Now you'll know what to look for. Remember, most people are good. There are still a lot of people you can trust.

How can I ever trust myself again?

You might feel that you made a terrible mistake. You trusted someone you shouldn't have. You liked someone who was mean to you. This may make you feel that you can't do anything right. You might start to feel that any decision you make will be wrong. But it wasn't your fault that someone you liked did something bad. And it doesn't mean that you're stupid. You were a victim. A crime is never the victim's fault.

Rape is an extremely traumatic experience. Rape damages the body and the emotions. While physical injuries will heal, emotional wounds take a longer time to heal, but it will happen. Here are some things you can do to help with the healing process:

One of the best things to do is to talk to someone about your feelings. You can speak with a professional counselor, or someone close to you, such as a friend or your parents.

It may be very difficult to open up to someone about what happened. You may feel ashamed, confused, and angered by what happened, but keeping these emotions bottled up will only make it harder to heal.

You can also *call a rape crisis center.* The person who answers the phone is an expert on rape. He or she will always believe you. Rape crisis counselors know all about date rape.

You can get the phone number of a rape crisis center by looking in the phone book under "Rape." Be sure to check both the white pages and the yellow pages. Or you can call the operator and ask to talk to a rape crisis center. When you call the rape crisis center, you can talk about anything you want. The counselor you talk to will never tell anyone what you said unless you want them to. The counselor will stay on the phone with you as long as you want. The counselor will help you *figure out exactly what happened to you.* She or he can give you advice about finding other people to talk to—a therapist, a minister or rabbi, a sympathetic friend, a parent.

Rape is against the law. You may decide you want to report your rape to the police.

Your rape crisis counselor can also help you decide about going to the police. Rape is against the law. You may decide you want to report your rape to the police. You may decide you want to take your case to court. It's your decision. If you decide to go to the police, your rape crisis counselor will be able to tell you what to expect.

Telling your story to strangers and being examined may be difficult, especially after such a traumatic experience, but keep in mind that it is necessary. If you decide to press charges, the police will need evidence. But even if you don't press charges, you will still need medical attention.

The police will take a report of what happened and open an investigation. You will need to go to a hospital. You will most likely go to a hospital where a doctor or nurse will examine you. The doctor will check for physical injuries and treat you if you have suffered physical injuries. The doctor will also collect evidence of the rape for the police. The doctor will also perform some tests. They will check for sexually transmitted disease and pregnancy. A counselor or social worker will be present if you need someone understanding and supportive to talk to.

You may also want legal help. Again your rape crisis counselor can tell you where to go. You will need to find a lawyer. But keep in mind that a trial will not be easy. You will need to tell your story in front of many people. Date rape is sometimes difficult to prove in court because many people still don't understand date rape. But that is beginning (and will continue) to change.

Recovering from date rape isn't easy, and it will take a long time. But recovery is possible. Many rape victims have recovered from their experience and gone on to live happy and successful lives. It can also happen to you. It takes patience, time, and hope.

If a friend has been raped, she may need you to listen.

Chapter 8

When a Friend Is Raped

If someone you love comes to you and says she has been raped, you may not know how to respond. Chances are you have never dealt with rape before and do not know what to say or do to comfort your friend. This chapter will give you some guidelines. Be there for her and listen to what she has to say. Just be a friend.

Empathize

Listen closely to what your friend tells you. She needs understanding and support at this difficult time. Although you may not know what to say to help her, what she may need is just someone to listen to her, understand, and comfort her.

Listen—a lot!

Date rape victims have a lot of confusing feelings.
Talking about those feelings will help a victim to
cope with them. She may need to talk about it for
a long time. She may need to talk about it more as
time goes by. You don't need to say much. She
just needs to know you're there.

Know how to get help.

If your friend tells you she's been raped, find out
what she's done about it. If she hasn't called a rape
crisis center, encourage her to. If she's been
injured, suggest she go to the hospital. If she wants
to go to the police, help her get advice at a rape
crisis center first. Date rape is very upsetting. Your
friend will probably need some help getting help.
You can help her do that.

Support her decisions.

If your friend doesn't want to go to the police,
don't make her. If she does want to go to the
police, help her do that. Date rape makes you
doubt your judgment. Friends should support a
victim's decisions. This will make the victim feel
more in control. It will make her feel more

The rape may even have happened years ago. But when the victim realizes what happened to her, she will need help.

confident. Don't try to force your friend to do anything. That will only make her think she *really* can't make decisions for herself.

It takes some date rape victims a long time to realize that they were raped. The rape may even have happened years ago. But when the victim realizes what happened to her, she will need help. She will need just as much support as someone who was raped more recently. Be the same kind of good friend to this kind of victim, too.

It's not easy to help a friend through a crisis. Especially when the crisis is something as awful as date rape. So be sure that *you* have support, too. Let someone know what *you're* going through. Otherwise, you might get upset and overwhelmed. Then you can't be a good friend. And if you feel that you're in over your head, get some advice from a rape counselor. She or he will tell you what to do next. You don't have to do this alone. Take care of yourself so you can take care of your friend.

Knowing the Facts

Date rape is a serious crime. It leaves victims hurt and confused, filled with a feeling of rage and betrayal that takes a long time to go away. Some survivors spend years trying to recover from the traumatic experience.

A lot of people mistakenly blame the victim of date rape. Some think she must have done something wrong or maybe she "led" the guy on. When someone is violated, and no one believes her, it only makes her feel worse. Very few reports of rape are false. It is something that not many people will lie about. Rape is never the victim's fault. It is a crime, and the criminal is at fault.

Knowing the facts about date rape will help you to understand how and why rape happens. It will also help you to see the truth behind the many myths that surround rape. Rape does not discriminate. Anyone can be a victim of rape. Survivors need support and understanding from everyone.

Glossary

acquaintance rape Forcing someone you know to have sex.

aggressive Pushy; being forceful to get what you want.

date rape Acquaintance rape that happens between two people who are dating.

feminine Having qualities that are regarded as characteristic of women or girls.

macho Like a "he-man"; tough.

media Newspapers, magazines, television, movies, radio, etc.

myth A belief not based on fact.

passive The opposite of aggressive; giving in to others.

rape Sex against someone's will.

rape crisis center A place where rape victims can get help.

rape crisis counselor A person trained to help rape victims.

sexual object Something that exists only for sexual pleasure.

stereotypes Common beliefs about what all members of a group are like. These beliefs may or may not be true in individual cases.

Where to Go for Help

Hospital Emergency Room
Ask if they have a Rape Trauma Team. This is a team of people who have special training in coping with rape.

Planned Parenthood Federation of America
810 Seventh Avenue
New York, NY 10019
(800) 230-7526
Web site: http://www.ppfa.org/ppga/

The Police
Dial 911 on any phone.

Rape Crisis Centers
Look in the white and/or yellow pages under crime victims' hotlines, rape, sexual assault services, or sex crimes report line.

The Rape, Abuse, and Incest National Network (RAINN)
252 10th St. N.E.
Washington, DC 20002
(800) 656-HOPE
Web site: http://www.rainn.org

Smart Date
P. O. Box 13232
San Luis Obispo, CA 93401
Web site: http://www.smartdate.com

For Further Reading

Bandon, Alexandra. *Date Rape.* Columbus, OH: Silver Burdett Press, 1994.

Bode, Janet. *The Voices of Rape.* New York: Franklin Watts, 1990.

Friedman, Joel, and Marcia Boumil. *Date Rape: What It Is, What It Isn't, What It Does to You, What You Can Do About It.* Deerfield Beach, FL: Health Communications, 1992.

Juke, Mavis. *It's a Girl Thing: How to Stay Healthy, Safe, and in Charge.* New York: Knopf, 1996.

Kaminker, Laura. *Everything You Need to Know About Dealing with Sexual Assault.* New York: The Rosen Publishing Group, 1998.

Levy, Barrie. *Dating Violence: Young Women in Danger.* Seattle, WA: Seal Press, 1991.

Mufson, Susan, and Rachel Kranz. *Straight Talk About Date Rape.* New York: Facts on File, 1997.

Parrot, Andrea, and Laurie Beehhofer. *Acquaintance Rape: The Hidden Crime.* New York: John Wiley & Sons, 1991.

——— . *Coping with Date Rape and Acquaintance Rape*, rev. ed. New York: The Rosen Publishing Group, 1995.

Stoppard, Miriam, Dr. *Sex Ed: Growing Up, Relationships, and Sex.* New York: DK Publishing, Inc., 1998.

Tamar, Erika. *Fair Game.* New York: Harcourt Brace, 1993.

Zvirin, Stephanie. *The Best Years of Their Lives: A Resource Guide for Teenagers in Crisis.* Chicago: American Library Association, 1992.

Index

About the Author
Frances Shucker-Haines is a freelance writer currently living in Ann Arbor, Michigan. She specializes in writing about parenting and child rearing.

About the Editor
Evan Stark is a well-known sociologist, educator, and therapist as well as a popular lecturer on women's and children's health issues. Dr. Stark was a Henry Rutgers Fellow at Rutgers University, an associate at the Institution for Social and Policy studies at Yale University, and a Fulbright Fellow at the University of Essex. He is the author of many publications in the field of family relations and is the father of four children.

Photo Credits
Cover and all inside photos by Stuart Rabinowitz.